Being
BEFORE
Doing

ALIGNING YOUR LIFE
WITH YOUR PURPOSE

KUDZAI SHOKO

Being Before Doing

ISBN: 9780620901260

Published by Nicholson Publishing

www.nicholsonic.co.za

NICHOLSON
PUBLISHING

CONTENTS

DEDICATION

This book is dedicated to my beautiful wife, Cleo and our blessed children, Zoe Danielle and Sean David. Your immeasurable support and patience have been commendable. HIS GRACE HAS SEEN US THROUGH. For this I am eternally grateful. May the Lord richly bless you beyond measure. Love, regards and respect!

FOREWORD

I am delighted that God told my son to write this book! The title intrigued me immediately and as I delved into it, I was deeply impressed with its thoughtfulness and depth. The challenges to living a Christ-like life have never been greater and this book is a valuable tool in living this life.

He makes a powerful argument for the idea that 'being' comes before 'doing', that what is of paramount importance in the life we wish or want to live, is first to know the Father and to live like Christ. The question of 'being' before 'doing' is the crux of the book; 'being' what and 'doing' what? The author explains the difference with infinite care and insight.

A Christian should be like Christ, live like Christ; going about his or her life like Christ. God is holy and He calls us to be holy. The essence of this is obvious if we are to do His work in His kingdom.

This book is a handbook, filled with guidelines and perceptions that are invaluable in our relationship with our Creator. It is filled with divine truth which the author has made highly accessible to every reader, not only Christians. He does this by sharing his own experiences in confronting the often difficult challenges the devil throws at us in living the Christ life.

The book is structured in such a way that the valuable lessons in each chapter are easy to grasp and apply. I am grateful to God for the writer, for the fact that my son gave his life to Christ and continuously strives to be more like the Lord he serves.

My prayer is that Kudzai's contribution to Christian literature will have a profound and lasting effect on the hearts of many people.

Mr. Bester Shoko

Grandpa to Zoe and Sean

INTRODUCTION

The title is really to convey a simple concept: it is necessary to understand your identity before embarking on your life-given purpose.

I define 'identity' as the focus on the character of the believer; simply put, this is knowing who we are in Christ. This is the 'being'. Once we truly know our identity, we are able to engage in our calling or vocation effectively and efficiently, successfully carrying out the 'doing'.

Christ residing in us enables the believer to 'do' life. So – welcome to 'Being before Doing'! I will seek to define and elaborate on concepts through analogies and illustrations, with the use of biblical text and motivational quotes. We will also look at topics such as time, implementation, fruition and reward. I hope that as you read, your own thoughts will be stimulated by your understanding of who you are (your 'being') and what you are called to do (your 'doing').

The book of all wisdom, the Bible, is the ultimate reference for those seeking a purposeful and well-lived life. It is therefore no surprise that "Being before Doing" is premised on biblical principles. The contents point to Jesus as the only Way, Truth and the Life.

Chapter 1

BEING

"An unexamined life is not worth living."

- Socrates

This book reflects experiences, principles and observations in the quest for a fulfilling life; a life that touches others and transforms them to be the best that they can be. It is premised on the principle that 'being precedes doing'.

A life is successful only in the measure to which it stands up to the scrutiny of those who have witnessed and experienced it. It is not necessarily a life without flaws or trouble, but one which has flourished despite these things. It is a life that is worth emulating and aspiring to. In the discussions we will examine personal experiences, not intended to humiliate or pressure others but rather to encourage by inspiration for transformation.

Many outstanding people are noted for their humble lives, their wise teachings that endure after them or their heroic exploits. Jesus Christ was known for his great works and teachings, but the record of his life gives us more than great traits to emulate. He gave us a template for living our lives.

Christ lived his life to manifest his purpose and not only was he a blessing to others, but he pleased God in all he did and said. He lived a perfect life and his legacy endures for all eternity. Jesus modelled a life of 'being before doing' – his existence was focused on his God-ordained purpose and nothing else.

It is interesting that not much is known about his early years except that they were determined by the law of God and a godly family environment.

However, we do know that his world, like ours, was far from perfect. He grew up under tumultuous socio-political circumstances and started his public ministry with great opposition from the phony religious establishment. He had tensions with his own family and a not-so-perfect team, but he still accomplished God's will for his life.

Jesus lived his life from the inside out. He knew who he was and why he had come. He was constantly guided by the Father who had sent him and did not deviate from that goal. There are three defining factors to his life that are critical to our understanding of 'being before doing'. These are framed in three statements that Jesus made around the time of his crucifixion.

FOR THIS REASON, I HAVE COME

"Now my heart is troubled, and what shall I say? 'Father, save me from this hour'? No, it was for this very reason I came to this hour. Father, glorify your name!" (John 12:27-28 NIV)

When he stood before Pilate and was being quizzed about his identity, his response was consistent. He came for a specific reason and that was not going to change;

"You are a king, then!" said Pilate. Jesus answered, "You are right in saying I am a king. In fact, for this reason I was born, and for this I came into the world, to testify to the truth. Everyone on the side of truth listens to me." (John 18:37 NIV)

His life was framed around a single mission. It was his guiding light. When he encountered the tempter, he was not swayed but stayed true to the mission. Most of us are easily persuaded away from the one main purpose of our lives and hence our lives do not turn out to be as compelling as Jesus' life was. Paul the apostle understood this: *"I count everything as dung so that I may grab hold of the calling to which he has called me." (Philippians 3:8)*

FATHER GLORIFY YOUR NAME

The second factor that distinguished the life of Jesus was that he was concerned with the glory of God. It did not matter what this took – he had his life staked out for the glory of God. In fact, this statement was uttered at a time when he was facing the most trying time of his life. Because he was born for this, he would glorify God through his obedience. Without a compelling God-glorifying vision, we cannot live a life that is outstanding.

IT IS FINISHED

Jesus made this statement and voluntarily gave up his spirit. He had accomplished the purpose and therefore had no more reason to hang on to life. That statement marked the end of his ministry at age 33. Just 3 years after bursting onto the scene! Many of us live very long and yet still find that purpose of God elusive or we lack the conviction to be sold out for it.

When we live a life that manifests purpose, we are not constrained to hold on to life. We do not fear the prospect of insignificance. We live from within.

Jesus said, *"No one takes (my life) from Me, but I lay it down of Myself. I have power to lay it down, and I have power to take it again" (John 10:18).* He was not trying to find his purpose by fumbling around and trying different options. He was living out his purpose and as a result, even when his purpose meant the termination of his life, he was not perturbed by it. He does not die with regret, fighting for one last chance!

In the following pages, I will ask you to consider the example of Jesus and invest in 'being' so that your 'doing' may result in God's will being accomplished in your life. This will also lead to a purposeful life that will be a blessing to others.

ONE REFLECTION

There are three aspects of Jesus Christ that are critical to our understanding of 'being before doing.' How did these challenge or affirm your own view of life?

Chapter 2

GOD'S BEING

"When man is restored to his true character, he recovers his original dominion. Now Christ is the image of God; therefore to be Christ's is to recover the original character which God created in man."

- Joseph S. Exell

Then God said, "Let Us make man in Our image, according to Our likeness; let them have dominion over the fish of the sea, over the birds of the air, and over the cattle, over [a]all the earth and over every creeping thing that creeps on the earth." So God created man in His own image; in the image of God He created him; male and female He created them. Then God blessed them, and God said to them, "Be fruitful and multiply; fill the earth and subdue it; have dominion over the fish of the sea, over the birds of the air, and over every living thing that moves on the earth." (Genesis 1:26 – 28)

Scripture explicitly says Man is made in the express image of God. Man's state of being is intriguing in every respect, particularly the fact that Man should mirror or reflect God. What an amazing and awesome thought. This fact is witness to the Godhead's approval and desire to have Man be the only unique being that represents God.

Man is therefore God's being. His life is complete in the life of God. God has expressed Man's existence through Himself. If God is spirit then Man is spirit. Man's uniqueness is that he is spiritual, simultaneously having a temporary natural experience on earth.

God is Spirit: and they that worship him, must worship him in spirit and in truth. (John 4:24)

Saint John helps us realise how unique our image in God is. Our being is the essence of God. It is the spirit of God breathed in Man. God's core is found nowhere in the universe or galaxy except in the existence of his chosen entity, Man.

Just how special is the being called Man? God not only mirrored His image with Man but created functional roles, male and female. These roles are so special because God planned to perpetuate creation through Man, in this way multiplying his image and filling the expanse of the earth. Earth is the territory given to Man to manifest God's glory.

God went further and bestowed his unconditional blessing on Man. In commanding that blessing, Man was given the responsibility of being fruitful and multiplying, replenishing, subjugating and ruling his surroundings.

Whilst God's record of the blessing is evident, strangely few walk in the full demonstration of this mandate. Writers, expository teachers of the Word of God and commentators have expressed much regarding how Man lost that authority of walking in the full blessing of God. A tragic episode in the Garden of Eden triggered a sorrowful beginning of the consequences of Man's high treason against the Godhead.

I sometimes imagine what life would have been if the union between God and Man had not been tampered with. Blessedly, God's restoration of Man is a perfect re-union post Man's fall in the Garden of Eden.

God is a Craftsman, Master-Planner, Genius of note. He placed his potential state of being in Man before Man did anything. He showed Man through instruction and blessing, command and rebuke, just what Man ought to epitomize.

In fact, God mandates Man with a state of being that reflects Him. Simply, God tells Man who he is supposed to be, and what to do. However, God looks to walk in relationship with Man regarding how to do things on Earth.

The faculties of the original man, Adam, were perfect in spirit, soul and body. God as perfection personified could only produce a perfect image of himself. What an amazing thought!

Man's fall replaced God's perfection with the wickedness of the devil and perversion entered humanity. Man, no longer reflected God; rather, he now reflected a fallen being, Satan. What a loss! Satan is everything that is the very antithesis of God. Thereafter, Man's motivation became contrary to God's mandate as commanded, blessed and instructed in Genesis.

The struggles of Man are recorded throughout the Bible. There is a great contrast between God's orderly way of being and Man's adopted and submitted way to the devil. However, even as Man groped his way towards a blessed life, God was preparing the Way of restoring his image in Man once again.

God in his grace and mercy provided the perfect mediator for restoration – his own son, Jesus Christ. Only he could restore us to the original image of God. However, although the spirit of Man is renewed instantly at the New Birth, the body and soul are not. (See John 3:16, Romans 10:8-10).

Our minds must undergo a process of renewal by using the Word of God. We must replace the 'corrupted files' in the mind to realign our thoughts with God's thinking.

Remember, Man lost his thinking as mandated by God. Fallen Man's thinking is heavily influenced by and open to Satan. As someone has said: 'The devil's thinking is stinking thinking'!

Man was originally ordained to think like God and, before his infamous fall, was in line with God's mandate. Thinking is like a lens that allows us to understand, visualize and interpret knowledge acquired. The thinking is not the challenge; it is the knowledge we think on that can create challenges. We could say that there is no such thing as a bad mind, but rather bad thoughts.

Our minds are a platform for processing thoughts, influenced by what we know, good or bad. Therefore, to have the mind of Christ means we must have knowledge of Christ and his being and his manner of doing things.

This is quite simply the Kingdom of God: God's thinking, and God's way of doing things.

Let's go back to Man's body; originally it was immortal. In order to carry God's image, the body had to be pure but Man's body became defiled at the Fall, because of sin. When we are born again, the body does not suddenly become immortal again. It is decaying constantly through age, sickness and disease. We need to look after the body as best we can and apply the Word of God to sustain it and combat decay.

Our bodies are to be preserved as worthy vessels for the Master's use, not abused and influenced by the devil. This is part of our redemption. We no longer belong to the devil but to Jesus Christ, the One who paid the purchase price for Man's salvation with His own precious, untainted blood.

LIFE'S LESSONS

My new birth took place some four decades ago. I was only a standard 1 pupil (Grade 3, aged 8) in a Catholic School, the top student of my class at the end of the first term that year.

For some miraculous reason, this achievement inspired my class teacher, Miss Sue Scott, to minister salvation to me during the morning school break.

After my confession of faith in the Lord Jesus Christ, she presented me with a Gideon's Bible and I signed my name on the designated page on the 13th April, 1975. I will forever be grateful to her.

Unfortunately, I had no-one to disciple me regarding the basics of Christian growth at that stage. I did not even know the basics of reading the bible let alone attending church until the 28th October 1990 when I visited a Pentecostal church for the first time in my life. My true journey of faith began then and through his Word, I am still growing in my relationship with God.

The journey has been graced with countless blessings and is never without challenges. So, I continue to ride the crest of life looking at deepening my relationship with this most awesome being, God. Everyone needs guidance in learning the ropes of relationships.

SOMEONE MUST BE YOUR PATH

The only path to God is Jesus Christ:

> *Jesus said to him, "I am the way, the truth, and the life. No one comes to the Father except through Me." (John 14:6)*

At the beginning of my walk with God, he changed my state of being, by transferring me from the kingdom of darkness to the Kingdom of light. Spiritually, I became a new babe in Christ that needed to grow.

I needed spiritual milk from the Word of God to mature. Unfortunately, in my environment there was no one to nourish me.

Being a new babe in Christ does not guarantee eventual maturity in Christ. Without the nourishment of the Word of God, even time will not produce growth! We need to be taught the Word of God. We need to know what it is to be a believer and operate in the believer's authority for ourselves.

Only 15 years after my spiritual birth did I begin to grow in God as I was nourished in his Word. Thank God for pastors and teachers of the Word of God. Thank God for local churches that diligently equip and train believers to be effective in the Kingdom.

I have continued being equipped and discipled for close on three decades. It is an enjoyable, challenging journey that has caused me to grow. During this period, God afforded me opportunities in church leadership, pioneering works, pastoring (running two branch churches) for 8 interesting years before moving me into the teaching ministry.

The theme of this book is 'becoming' before 'doing'. Getting to know God and how we reflect him is paramount before we try to do great and mighty works. It is relationship first.

I am reminded of the text from the New Testament:

"Therefore whoever hears these sayings of Mine, and does them, I will liken him to a wise man who built his house on the rock: and the rain descended, the floods came, and the winds blew and beat on that house; and it did not fall, for it was founded on the rock. But everyone who hears these sayings of Mine, and does not do them, will be like a foolish man who built his house on the sand: and the rain descended, the floods came, and the winds blew and beat on that house; and it fell. And great was its fall." And so it was, when Jesus had ended these sayings, that the people were astonished at His teaching, for He taught them as one having authority, and not as the scribes. (Matthew 7:24-29)

In life, believers need to move according to the speed of faith. In our quest to arrive somewhere quickly, we are not willing to be thorough in the foundation, direction and what it takes in life to pursue our journey of life, often referred to as our destiny. Like someone said, 'Haste makes waste.' It took some time for me to get to know 'my being' in Christ before I could successfully contribute to Kingdom effectiveness.

From my experience, becoming a Christian was a result of deciding to be a child of God, through Jesus Christ. This supernatural transformation did not require my effort but was a result of receiving salvation at Christ's expense.

However, to become an effective Christian effectively needed a growth process of nourishment from the Word. My 'being' came from being taught, learning and doing God's Word.

I am amazed that even within our earthly education systems wisdom and common sense suggest the importance of a formation process of 'being' before 'doing'. So, for the most part of 13 years of schooling, I learnt about 'becoming' before I had the opportunity of 'doing'.

While the 'doing' part is usually a job, an assignment or a calling, the 'becoming' part is the character development. 'Becoming' in life will always precede 'doing'. My advice is just this: learn and prepare 'who you are' well and you will execute 'who you are' in life well. Let me emphasise this – you reap what you put into life. An ill-prepared life is to be avoided and is difficult to overcome.

So, find out who you are. It is your life's vocation, purpose and calling. Continuously develop a character that is fitting for your life's vocation because the kingdom needs you urgently!

In the seeking to become, our potential should be harnessed by thorough preparation and process. Unfortunately, there is no pre-life to practice life. Life demands on the job training. Life is an incredible crucible, the experiences of which cannot be confined to classrooms of teaching, coaching and training alone.

Life must just be lived! In preparing for life, one needs to find the balance between extreme and insignificant living. Generally, anything extreme attracts error no matter how good it maybe. So, look to live a balanced life.

In acknowledging that preparation is a vital cog for daily living, someone wisely said, 'If we do not plan, we plan to fail.' Another suggested that when we don't prepare, the things we hoped would not happen, do happen.

Without a compelling vision or life vocation, preparation is a futile exercise. The fact that our lives here on earth can be hustled and bustled by frenetic activity does not guarantee progressive living. Finding out who you are is crucial before you engage in what you are called to do.

However, some activity *is* necessary to accomplish our calling. Consequently, there is a definite need to know our purpose in life before engaging in the works of that purpose.

Preparation is a powerful tool in realising our dreams and life's callings. Jesus epitomises this perfectly. Thirty years of all kinds of development preceded his three and a half years of ministry here on earth.

Preparation helps build our capacity to be effective in carrying out the tasks and vocations of our lives. Preparation builds character in anticipation of what needs to manifest. Preparation is like a magnet that draws out the essence of life from the mediocrity of cluttered living.

A vision which is thoroughly prepared knows how to separate the perfect from the permissible. In fact, focused preparation creates the opportunity to achieve its desired purposes.

Some who knew the prophetic message of the Messiah may have become anxious because Jesus seemed to be biding his time in taking up His ministry. They may genuinely wondered just when he would save the world from its separation from God.

The 30 years Jesus spent in obscurity was never lost time. Rather, it prepared him thoroughly for what lay ahead. He diligently watched and waited in obedience, finding favour with God and mankind.

Between his appearance as a baby in swaddling clothes lying in a manger in Bethlehem and his ascension to heaven, there is a remarkable process through various stages of development. Each stage in his life marked progress towards fulfilling his purpose.

The biblical account of the time after his Jewish Bar Mitzvah recounts no major events, only hinting at him working in a carpenter's shop. The conspicuous gap between the ages of 13 and 30 is pregnant with the hidden process.

We can only imagine the details of Jesus' daily life. What was the significance of this period? Sometimes the process of life may seem to suggest that nothing is taking place. However, often these seemingly insignificant periods in life build an internal capacity for the execution of what lies ahead.

A tree in winter may look lifeless; yet a cross-section of its trunk would show the growth rings of increasing strength. The tree looks dead, the leaves fall off and there is no obvious growth. However, in the hidden place, where no eye can see, the roots are deepening and storing vital food for the trees. So it is with the winters of our lives. There is growth but it is unseen!

In this amazing season of dormancy, the trees go through cyclic phases of rest – early rest, winter rest and after rest. Each phase is marked by a distinct set of physiological processes.

By observing the cyclic nature of the development of trees we can understand the transition between different phases. Most are gradual rather than instant, much like the amazing process that produces a human being. It begins with a sperm fertilising an ovum in a woman's womb and ultimately culminates in an adult. It is truly miraculous!

Ignoring human developmental processes can be detrimental to how a person turns out. Therefore, it makes sense that ignoring the process of being God's creation can have an adverse effect here on earth and eternity later. Man is a being of decisions, process and preparation.

The integration of process and preparation in life is vital in Man's 'being'. The term 'human being' was never intended to be limiting. In God's original creation design it was meant to show our unlimited potential. God's intention for humanity in this regard has still not changed.

ONE REFLECTION

Preparation happens in the background, but it is preceded by a clarity of assignment. What values do we learn while we are being prepared for our purpose?

Chapter 3

GOD'S DOING

"Jesus said to them, "Have you never read in the Scriptures: 'The stone which the builders rejected has become the chief cornerstone. This was the Lord's doing, and it is marvelous in our eyes'?"

- Matthew 21:42

The creation of Man is a product of God's own awesome thoughts. He then translated those thoughts into action and formed Man. His intention was never to be rejected but embraced by Man in fellowship that is eternal. Man belongs to God.

In the English Thesaurus, the word 'doing' is a synonym of action, deed and feat. 'Doing' is the verb of the spoken word. I like to say that anything not worth speaking is not worth doing! Doing is also the manifestation of the intents and thoughts of the heart.

I am amazed at my denial at times, when I have said something foolish and then try to negate it by saying, 'I did not mean to say that.' Nothing is done that was not first a thought. As always, God is our perfect example – he never does anything without having purposed it. 'Doing' is an outward manifestation of purpose. God is purposeful and so Man, as God's expressed image, should also be purposeful.

In the previous chapter we discussed the fact that Man belongs to God. Out of that conversation I will also state Man must 'become' before 'doing'. Built on this premise Man is designed to be a 'doer' just like His Master.

Despite the fall of Man, God still seeks to trust Man because He made Man as a trust-worthy being, just like himself. That is why a 'righteous' man, meaning one in 'right standing with God', may fall but has the ability to get back up again.

You cannot put a righteous person down, unless they choose not to get back up again. As long as we are righteous before God, we are worthy to be trusted by God. Let us put the above into context: we need to know that we can be trusted. Whilst our spirits are transformed into the Kingdom of light, our minds need renewal to understand this transformation.

What forms our thinking outside of God needs to be renewed with a Kingdom way of thinking that is in direct alignment with God's way of thinking. If we can think like God, we are ready to be trusted by God and to do things like God.

The way we think impacts heavily on what we do. A non-believer's way of thinking is contrary to God's way. A believer without a renewed mind in line with God's way of thinking is a baby in the things of God. A believer with a renewed mind in line with God's way of thinking is a mature person doing the will and purpose of God. Such a person becomes fit to represent God here on earth effectively.

God always starts with the end in mind. He makes startling statements to various characters in the Bible. He calls a childless father and mother parents to many nations. He calls a Hebrew child, drawn from the water escaping the wrath of an Egyptian Pharaoh's decree to kill all baby boys, to deliver the nation of Israel from 430 years of bondage.

He calls an orphaned winner of a beauty pageant to become queen to save a chosen nation in Susa. He calls a shepherd boy, who despite not even being invited to a prophet's anointing parade of a future king, to be king of

Israel. Many stories in the Bible depict people born in a disadvantaged predicament.

However, they overcame because they were designed for greatness in God's kingdom. Paul the Apostle echoes that when he writes to the Corinthian believers:

> *Brothers, think of what you were when you were called. Not many of you were wise by human standards; not many were influential; not many were of noble birth. But God chose the foolish things of the world to shame the wise; God chose the weak things of the world to shame the strong. He chose the lowly things of this world and the despised things — and the things that are not — to nullify the things that are, so that no one may boast before him.*
> *(1 Corinthians 1:26-30 NIV)*

It is not where you are born, but rather who you are in God that becomes the crux of the matter. Can you imagine the calling of Joseph who was a rather spoilt child, Jacob's favourite, always ready to spill the beans on his brothers' escapades when tending to their father's herds? His father even designed a special coat that clearly set him apart as being favoured above his siblings.

This story of Joseph is well known. It began with Joseph's dream and his boastful talk regarding his destiny. This inevitably led to conflict with his siblings, who could no longer tolerate him and wanted to get rid of him. They schemed to kill him, stripping him of his coat of many colours and throwing him into a pit until they could come up with a viable plan.

The brothers finally decided to sell him off to Egyptian traders and then lied to Jacob, their father, saying that he had been killed by some ravenous animal. Understandably, Jacob tore his clothes in grief and deeply mourned the death of his favourite son.

Meanwhile, Joseph experienced life-transforming phases leading towards a God-designed and God-ordained destiny. He found favour with Potiphar, the Egyptian ruler, and worked for him. However, it didn't take long for Potiphar's wife also to notice him and try to seduce him. When he resisted her, she accused him of attempted rape, branding him, landing him in prison!

In prison he found favour with the wardens and inmates. Now his God-given ability to interpret dreams became an asset. He was able to interpret the dreams of his fellow inmates – the cupbearer would be restored to his position; the baker would be condemned to death.

Sadly, the cupbearer now forgot all about Joseph until the day Pharaoh became troubled by his own dreams and called for interpreters. It took a while for the cupbearer to remember his former cellmate but after repeated attempts by others to interpret Pharaoh's dreams, the convict was called in.

Joseph no longer was full of himself but immediately acknowledged his God, who had given him the ability to interpret dreams. He successfully revealed to Pharaoh the meaning of his dreams.

It could be that the best he hoped for now was better prison conditions but, wonderfully, Pharaoh recognised Joseph's gift and its possible impact on his future leadership. He was able to recognise Joseph's potential and made him his second in charge, the equivalent of Prime Minister of Egypt.

"Eye has not seen, nor ear heard, nor have entered into the heart of man the things which God has prepared for those who love Him." (1Corinthians 2:9)

Joseph developed character, integrity and reputation through challenging life experiences. He was now able to see beyond self-advancement and sought to reconcile with his family. His earlier arrogance was replaced by compassion for his brothers that took him beyond his personal agenda to submitting to God's agenda for Israel.

Famine visited not only Egypt but its surroundings including Jacob and his household, and his family went in search of relief from Egypt. There they once again encountered Joseph. How awed they must have been at his position of influence! Eventually there was a family reconciliation and because of Joseph, the family had access to the best Egypt had to offer, even during famine.

Joseph executed his duties diligently. He 'became' before he 'did'. What was placed inside of him by God was of greater consequence to what he needed to do and his relationship with God was key in his calling. Do not underestimate what lies within you. Yes, my friend, greatness lies within you and creation is waiting for the manifestation of that which God has placed in you.

For the earnest expectation of the creation eagerly waits for the revealing of the sons of God. For the creation was subjected to futility, not willingly, but because of Him who subjected it in hope; because the creation itself also will be delivered from the bondage of corruption into the glorious liberty of the children of God. For we know that the whole creation groans and labors with birth pangs together until now. (Romans 8:19-22)

Joseph typifies many of us when we start off in a relationship with God. We are wearing coats foreign to God's design and intention for our lives. It is possible to have a selfish dream or desire in the name of God. Just like Joseph, we may have not sought God's plan and purpose in our lives. Joseph encountered a stripping of garments along the way; in his quest to do God's purpose, he was stripped of some things. His original many-coloured coat pointed to the favouritism of his earthly father.

In stripping Joseph of this coat, the enemy thought he would strip him of his father's favour. I believe that in the pit God replaced that lost coat with his favour, because Joseph prospered immediately upon arriving in Potiphar's house. Symbolically, when Potiphar's wife grabbed at Joseph's garment in lust, she attempted to strip him of his 'coat' of character, integrity, calling, destiny for success and his dreams.

Character is more important to God than it is to us. Joseph sought character above the reputation before Man. This is non-negotiable with God. He works on us in apparent obscurity, but it is in his presence that we are made. God takes pleasure in being alone with us, building us for his purpose and his glory.

In Joseph's encounter in prison God showed him the divine dream for his destiny. The enemy will try and strip you of what represents you here on earth, but he cannot access who you represent – the Greater One on the inside of you.

When the enemy seeks to strip, God is always at hand to clothe you with his compassion, grace and faith.

Joseph kept his focus on God, never disowning him. His challenges were no longer bigger than his God. In stripping off his prison clothing, I sincerely believe God's approval was ushered in for purposed service for his kingdom. God, through Pharaoh, dressed Joseph with a ring of authority and the new garments of rulership, wisdom and revelation, representing Joseph's destiny, calling and restoration by God.

LIFE'S LESSONS

Jesus, Mighty God, Wisdom, Deliverer, Lion of the Tribe of Judah, Word of Life, Advocate, Provider, The Great I Am, Helper, Savior, Prince of Peace, Wonderful Counselor, Lamb of God, Lord of Hosts, Root of David, Author and Finisher of our Faith, The Way, Healer, Son of God, The Truth, Chief Cornerstone, King of Kings, Light of the World, Chief Shepherd, My Strength and Song, Righteous Judge, Son of Righteousness, Resurrection and Life, The Alpha and Omega.

As I meditate on some of the things Jesus is and what he manifested here on earth, I am left with an awesome responsibility to be and do what God has ordained. There are just not enough words to describe Jesus, to reveal both who he is and what he did, what he does and what he will keep doing.

In seeking to do right, there are some lessons we can learn from others. I came across this prayer of St. Francis of Assisi, which I thought ministers fittingly to the heart in relating to God.

> Lord, make me an instrument of Thy peace;
> Where there is hatred, let me sow love;
> Where there is injury, pardon;
> Where there is doubt, faith;
> Where there is despair, hope;
> Where there is darkness, light;
> And where there is sadness, joy.
> O Divine Master,
> Grant that I may not so much seek to be consoled as to console;
> To be understood, as to understand;
> To be loved, as to love;
> For it is in giving that we receive,
> It is in pardoning that we are pardoned,
> And it is in dying that we are born to Eternal Life.
> Amen.

I trust that this prayer inspires you to be guided by God's essentials for living and doing His will.

"Leaders are created in the crucible of life, not a classroom." Wisdom for the ages: Drew.

Although this quote addresses leaders, it is actually appropriate to people from all walks of life. Everyone is likely to lead at some point somewhere. Mulling over what has happened in my life, I have come to believe that leadership can be taught through coaching and training but life needs to be lived today! I must confess – life has not always been easy for me. It has had its twists and turns, its bends in the road, and it is not over yet. I have no doubt that you too have experienced this.

There are some things that I would ask God. Why do I have to do this? Why did I go there? Why will I have to go through this? Somewhere in my thinking I have registered the fact that life is about being and doing what you are called to be. Just like writing this book.

If I had known, maybe I could have tried to bargain with God for a different assignment. Writing this book was not my idea but his idea. Where I was in life did not stop him instructing me to write this book. He is more concerned about who you are than where you are in life. I was looking for an excuse to wrangle my way out of this responsibility.

I seek to write and say whatever we are called to live for. This requires an intimate relationship with the Giver of Life. Disobedience to his instruction in our lives results in lives that are futile. Obedience on the other hand means fulfilling the design of the Master's intent for our lives. At the conclusion of our lives, will you and I hear, 'Well done good and faithful servant?' or the opposite, 'Depart from me for I never knew you, you evil and slothful servant', and be banished to eternal damnation.

In my continued quest to understand more of the full Counsel of God's Word, the following traits seem to visit Man here on earth. Sometimes, not of our own doing or lack of obedience, God allows us through arid places. I think of Jesus being led by the Spirit into the wilderness to be tried and tempted by the devil. Although I haven't had exactly this experience, I have been deeply challenged.

Challenges tend to bring about change. Change is inevitable in life and yet many are never prepared for it. I have observed that change is now a constant factor in my life! Initially, I loathed the very fact of the need to change. I soon realised that the catalysts for change bring growth. Do I want to grow? Yes, but am I willing to pay the price for such growth? That is another story. Anyway, change has become acceptable, as I constantly seek to negotiate with the Master as he moulds, reconstructs and renews my life.

I say 'negotiated' because I have emotionally and tearfully been gripped by the manifestation of God's presence and gone to him and asked, 'Lord have your way in my life and Lord do what you desire in me.' This sounds so super-spiritual, yet, when change arrived, I wanted to run away, binding the enemy. Nevertheless, the Lord took me at my word. This resulted in a 'life pause' which seemed dry, lacking direction. Yet in spiritual reality, God was patiently waiting to re-engage me on my earlier request to transform me. Eventually, by the Spirit of God, I have gotten back to the agenda for change.

Whilst the process itself may not seem remarkable; the result has been supernatural. Jesus' wilderness experience was not spectacular but was supernatural. He overcame the enemy by the written Word of God. Does putting the Word of God in your life seem spectacular? Not always. Yet it yields supernatural results when released into our lives by faith. There are different perceptions of the wilderness experience but one thing that is sure: God graciously manifests his word for that experience.

Time preparing for a vision to manifest seems beyond all comprehension. Time is an endless currency that allows us to repetitiously train towards desired outcomes but unfortunately cannot be stored. So, we must use time wisely. Therefore, it is just not safe to say how much time we have on this earth but rather what value we seek out of the time available. Time is the commodity that is required to bring about the process of transformation in our lives.

Some seem to require more time that others, depending on the gravity of the assignment. Nevertheless, God needs time with us. It is a commodity earmarked as a currency to be spent wisely here on earth. I have never thought of life as being boring. At times, I do hear people talk about being bored with life. I would like to think one ought to have a fulfilling life and I believe vision provides that spur, that inspiration and incentive for living.

'An investment in knowledge pays the best interest.'
Benjamin Franklin

We are witnesses to a world that is relentless in its quest for information. The thirst for knowledge is phenomenal. Whether technology, communication or new discoveries, the pace increases after each conquest of some new frontier. Yet in all this, motivated as we are, we fall way short in dealing with the challenges of humanity. For instance, by far the majority of earth's population is steeped in poverty, yet most of its resources are available to only 20% of its population. This is just one of many deep-seated problems.

To say the least, we do not seem to understand or have little knowledge regarding the root causes of the evil manifestation of earth's lack. The selling of bad news becomes the order of the day, whilst good news is slotted in occasionally as a sop to our consciences.

Have we, in pursuit of living, lost the motivation to love God and love our neighbour, as Jesus commanded? Do we turn a blind eye to suffering and instead tuck into the feast of greed, selfishness and purposelessness that our society supplies at every turn? The world has invested hugely in knowledge; however, the interest of that investment has not bettered the lives of humanity. There is therefore something inherently evil in the rich getting richer and the poor getting poorer. The systems of living in the world oppose the Kingdom of God.

The world's curriculum for life has fared dismally against the Kingdom way of doing life. Governments have for centuries shunned the principled Kingdom of God as a way of living. Surely now is the opportune time to turn to God's Way of doing 'earth' – 'Thy kingdom come, Thy will be done.' Oh yes, let it come!

Having failed dismally in running the matters here on earth, we must surely realise that our state of 'being' has not enhanced our 'doing'. Some may disagree with my portrayal of human failure. In response I would say, we have been efficient with the non-essentials of life. Collectively, we have not pitched up purposefully. Our self-will has been tested severely by the world systemic approach to life. Man continues to grind out in search of far-fetched dreams of paradise, only an illusion, surrounded by disarray, dismay, depression, pessimism and all its cousins.

Worldwide TV news beams little encouragement, support or sustenance of life befitting humanity. Yet again we shun the Gospel, the good news, a promise of love, hope and faith. The promise is for every 'being' called by God. The promise is for every 'doer' of the Word of God. This is the God that created the universe. In our failure to worship him, our 'being' still seeks to worship things that we have dominion, authority and power over. Our misunderstanding, frustration and ego continue as if it were a test before God.

This reveals to us that we have not understood God. In St Francis' prayer, we have not sought to understand God before we could be understood. I guess in all this, it makes us understand that as 'beings' we need Almighty God. As 'doers' mandated by God's Word may we endure what life continues to relentlessly throw at us. It is our attitude towards life that can either negatively or positively impact us and our neighbours. It is time to make the believer's influence felt!

The manifestation of 'doers' on earth is a result of the tests of life. Tests help 'doers' manifest a systematic way that emanates from our 'being'. In an attempt to get on with life, the Designer of life has only provided One Way, a way that allows no compromise.

There is a way that seems right to a man,
But its end is the way of death. (Proverbs 14:12)

In the way of righteousness is life, And in its
pathway there is no death. (Proverbs 12:28)

In our state of 'being' and 'doing', we need to be mindful of what the Word of God cautions. Have you chosen your own way or are you unaware of the Way? Seek God; find his Way in his Word. God has a way of processing those in service to his kingdom. He is like a potter at his wheel making clay vessels for use. He prepares us by crushing and forming us, moulding us into vessels fit for his use (becoming and doing). What type of person are you becoming as a result of the process?

There are four groups of people in life with only one that would effectively describe God's kingdom:

1. *Wrong people doing the wrong things*
2. *Right people doing the wrong things*
3. *Wrong people doing the right things*
4. *Right people doing the right things*

Which group do you represent?

ONE REFLECTION

God's purpose unfolds in stages.
Sometimes we are not aware what is
happening until we look back and see
the path we have walked.
What are the different stages that you
can identify in your life journey?
What are you doing now in what you
understand as God's purpose for your
life?

Chapter 4

TIMING

"All of the great leaders have had one characteristic in common: it was the willingness to confront unequivocally the major anxiety of their people in their time."

- John Kenneth Galbraith

Amazingly, time is an interesting commodity that can court fascination and controversy at the same instance. Science, the Arts, Religion and others have sought to define time through their respective lenses. Each perspective carries a processed theory that endeavours to be credible and have merit. I don't consider myself to be expert enough to say which theory is the most appropriate. However, for the purpose of our study I will look at time through a generalised lens so as to appeal to as wide an audience as possible.

> *"Time is a part of the measuring system used to sequence events, to compare the durations of events and the intervals between them, and to quantify rates of change such as the motions of objects. The temporal position of events with respect to the transitory present is continually changing; future events become present, then pass further and further into the past. Time has been a major subject of religion, philosophy, and science, but defining it in a non-controversial manner applicable to all fields of study has consistently eluded the greatest scholars."*
> *- Wikipedia*

The definition above seeks to knit together all perceptions regarding time. From a Judeo-Christian point of view, time is linear, starting with God's creation, with the end of the world as final destination. We also know that this approach needs to take eternity into consideration.

Time can be better understood from two words in the Greek Language, *'Chronos'* and *'Kairos'*. *'Chronos'* gives us the word chronology; this speaks numerically regarding the sequential nature or order of time, the measured element of time connected to instances and episodes of life.

'*Kairos*' on the other hand refers to the nature of time as being divine and qualitative. It speaks about epoch, era, and period, designed with events, significance and even prophetic moments in mind.

In particular, the Old Testament time in the Bible is for the most part, traditionally regarded as a medium for the passage of predestined events. In the New Testament we see time more consistently being linear, highlighting events, purpose and prophecy.

The dynamics of time are interesting, so much so that King Solomon, in the Old Testament book Ecclesiastes, writes the following:

To everything there is a season,
A time for every purpose under heaven:

> *A time ito be born,*
> *And a time to die;*
> *A time to plant,*
> *And a time to pluck what is planted;*
> *A time to kill,*
> *And a time to heal;*
> *A time to break down,*
> *And a time to build up;*
> *A time to weep,*
> *And a time to laugh;*
> *A time to mourn,*
> *And a time to dance;*

A time to cast away stones,
And a time to gather stones;
A time to embrace,
And a time to refrain from embracing;
A time to gain,
And a time to lose;
A time to keep,
And a time to throw away;
A time to tear,
And a time to sew;
A time to keep silence,
And a time to speak;
A time to love,
And a time to hate;
A time of war,
And a time of peace. (Ecclesiastes 3:1-8)

King Solomon is speaking about the Kairos moments in a human being's lifetime. These moments will obviously carry the chronological time.

King Solomon hints that each lifetime has a 'best before date' prior to the expiry of Kairos time. In order to effectively demonstrate the desirable as commissioned beings of the Kingdom of God, there is a need to understand the process of 'becoming' before 'being'.

In our discussion of time we are always engaging a series of activities captured in this space called time. This brings me to the element of timing in life. Just what is timing?

'Timing is the time when something happens or the spacing of events in time.' (Wikipedia)

The Merriam-Webster's Dictionary gives the definition of the word 'timing' as a noun in three facets as follows:

Placement or occurrence in time (the timing of the sale could not have been better)
The ability to select the precise moment for doing something for optimum effect (a boxer with impeccable timing)
Observation and recording (as by a stopwatch) of the elapsed time of an act, action, or process.

Let's look at this in more depth below.

LIFE'S LESSONS

In the Bible, Daniel understood from the books the number of years certain prophetic moments and events were to take place. These times were ordained in Bible history for a purpose that would impact the Kingdom of God.

Daniel was a character who featured prominently in the Babylonian Courts. Whilst educated in a Chaldean culture, he embraced wisdom from God, interpreting visions and dreams. He himself also had apocalyptic visions.

Daniel was in captivity but he remembered Jeremiah the Prophet's words predicting 70 years of captivity and bondage. He studied God's recorded Word, not the secular writings of his time and sought to understand the times, particularly, God's times.

Daniel understood who he was. Through study he had 'become' in God and now sought 'being'. He sought purpose for his time, knowing that his people would go back to Jerusalem after 70 years of captivity.

This is a demonstration of a man linking knowledge to reality. He linked knowledge, wisdom and understanding to the apportioned timing of a prophetic word. In his world he used what he knew, together with what was happening around him in his day.

The Word says Daniel set his face towards God. He changed his focus towards his Source, making God the centre of his life. He demonstrated this by aligning and repositioning himself with God's prophetic word.

Daniel was remarkable as he stood proxy and prayed on behalf of Israel. He did not seek his own agenda, but rather God's agenda of the time. Timing was crucial for Daniel as his life's purpose stirred him to respond to a Prophetic Action corresponding to a Prophetic Word.

Timing in God seems to be determined by his seasons and his purposes. Just like the returning of Jesus, the timing is decreed by God not Man. God seeks to work with Man regarding timing of occurrences, events and prophecy.

It seems that God's process prepares us for a cause that substantiates the propagating of the Kingdom of God. Kairos and Chronos work together regarding God's timing to accomplish the tasks at hand. It makes for interesting reading. Just how accurate is God's timing for events, occurrences and prophecies?

The Bible records various covenants between God and Abraham. One in particular records Abraham in a trance when God spoke to him regarding Israel's future captivity. Bible history reveals God's Word as a certainty; so is God's timing a certainty.

At times, even in my own life, I have misunderstood the timing of God. Jesus predicted for us seasons of prosperity and tribulations as a certainty. Yet, we rarely are ever prepared for the challenging season. Somehow, it looks like we live in a one-dimensional world while God operates in 3-D.

We seek to pray away God's certainty of a turbulent world in the end-times in exchange of an illusion of comfort, which is like seeking to catch a mirage on a scorching summer's day. God determines the times of nations and dispensations and we can determine our preparation in response.

Do we know where God is right now or are we in pursuit of our own agenda? And are we seeking God's endorsement of that agenda? Whilst I am a firm believer in the faith message, you can't 'faith away' God's plan and purpose for you having to go through the fiery furnace. Remember the three Hebrew boys? It was God's purpose for them to experience the 'fiery furnace'.

In our becoming, faith must be a component that helps us relate with God intimately. Faith must not be something to just acquire 'stuff' from God. Faith is not to be demonstrated as a hoarding exercise but as a propagation of the purposes of God.

Israel's original captivity and bondage was 400 years. However, Israel's actual years of captivity became 430 years. What happened? Having been delayed from 400 years to 430 years (something went wrong with Moses the liberator).

Now it came to pass in those days, when Moses was grown, that he went out to his brethren and looked at their burdens. And he saw an Egyptian beating a Hebrew, one of his brethren. So he looked this way and that way, and when he saw no one, he killed the

*Egyptian and hid him in the sand. And when he went
out the second day, behold, two Hebrew men were
fighting, and he said to the one who did the wrong,
"Why are you striking your companion?"
Then he said, "Who made you a prince and a judge
over us? Do you intend to kill me as you killed the
Egyptian?"
So Moses feared and said, "Surely this thing is known!"
When Pharaoh heard of this matter, he sought to kill
Moses. But Moses fled from [a]the face of Pharaoh
and dwelt in the land of Midian; and he sat down by a
well. (Exodus 2:11-15)*

Moses may have understood the timing for Israel's
liberator as they drew closer to 400 years. However, he had
not 'become' before 'doing' and he did not have God's
method. Obviously, his Hebrew brothers did not recognise
Moses as the liberator.

There is a 30-year discrepancy between what the Lord
told Abram and what it says in Exodus. If we take the 40 years
Moses spent in the wilderness (Acts 7:30) from 430 years,
the actual time the children of Israel came out of Egypt, we
are left with 390 years. Could it be that the disparity occurred
because the killing of the Egyptian by Moses of the Egyptian
was actually a premature attempt to liberate the Israelites in
the 390th year of their captivity? Could it be that Moses

missed God's timing, plan and purpose by being 10 years ahead of God's schedule? (Also reference Habakkuk 2:2-4)

Vision carries God's timing not Man's perceived readiness and preparation. Getting ahead of God showed Moses' impatience, resulting in 40 years in the desert. He could have waited out 10 years aligning it to 400 years as prophesied to Abram. God is precise when it comes to vision and timing. I am convinced that a large part of this is attributed to the intense preparation of people, places, plans and provision. Being out of sync with this has the potential to be perilous. It's worth noting that the Bible shows God preparing Abram for 27 years before the manifestation of Isaac, the child of promise. Joseph also endured 22 years before ascending to the position of Prime Minister to Pharaoh in Egypt. Saul, who became Paul, journeyed 14 years in his establishment of what God had called him for. It is vitally important to clearly understand that when God calls you, you yield to His plan, timing and purpose. You will do well not go ahead of God as Moses did.

It is therefore key and critical that one has God's Word, instruction and the leading of the Holy Spirit when doing God's will for your life. The 'hand of flesh' cannot supersede the Spirit of God in destiny issues as predestined and ordained by the Sovereign God. We dare not forget this! When it comes to God's timing, you cannot speed him up. You do not have the capability that he does to create order.

Remember, he is Omni-present, Omniscient and Omnipotent. I am learning to yield to him no matter what it looks like.

The Israelites only saw a murderer. They did not understand God's timing for Exodus. It took Moses another 30 years beyond the original 400 years to lead the exodus of the Israelites from Egypt.

> *Now when he was forty years old, it came into his heart to visit his brethren, the children of Israel. And seeing one of them suffer wrong, he defended and avenged him who was oppressed, and struck down the Egyptian. For he supposed that his brethren would have understood that God would deliver them by his hand, but they did not understand. And the next day he appeared to two of them as they were fighting, and tried to reconcile them, saying, 'Men, you are brethren; why do you wrong one another?' But he who did his neighbor wrong pushed him away, saying, 'Who made you a ruler and a judge over us? Do you want to kill me as you did the Egyptian yesterday? Then, at this saying, Moses fled and became a dweller in the land of Midian, where he had two sons. And when forty years had passed, an Angel of the Lord appeared to him in a flame of fire in a bush, in the wilderness of Mount Sinai. (Acts 7:23-30)*

The above scriptures reinforce what transpired in the Book of Exodus. The Israelites did not understand God's timing. They lived without understanding the times God had apportioned them.

It is in this respect that 'becoming' before 'doing' becomes an imperative in God's timing and his seasons. Have we become victims who suffer from something that we do not understand? Do we recognise the prophetic season and God's clock for our life?

Ever since grasping what I have shared with you, I constantly question myself; 'Do I, Kudzai Shoko, understand my day of God's visitation?'

I encourage you to do the same. Let's take our example from those who did great exploits, men and women who understood God's day of visitation. The day, moment and or season is when God reveals to us his plan and purpose specifically for the Kingdom of God's advancement. May the Lord help all of us!

I love David. He was a man after God's heart yet he exhibited appalling character flaws – adultery, murder and attempting to conceal his sin. Yet he repented of all this. His integrity was not about being right or wrong, but rather in reconciling with the truth.

This son in God's kingdom recognised the season of God's visitation in his illustrious life. He continued working on becoming God's man. Israel could have been so caught up in captivity and bondage that they missed their season of God's visitation. Timing and a heroic slaughter of a giant changed the course of Israel's history with the Philistines.

I have vowed that I will not miss the season of God's visitation. My continent Africa must not miss her destiny and season of God's visitation. If the Sons of Issachar understood the signs of the times, I am confident that we too can understand these signs and prepare adequately.

Timing in another context speaks of God's appointment for certain things that need to be done. God seems to have a 'shelf-life' or 'best before date' for purpose to be revealed and executed. Stepping out to do God's purpose prematurely can result in disaster.

> For the vision is yet for an appointed time;
> But at the end it will speak, and it will not lie.
> Though it tarries, wait for it;
> Because it will surely come,
> It will not tarry. (Habakkuk 2:3)

Vision in God is for an appointed time, simply because God is the God of order. God's timing is impeccable and undisputable. In our fallibility, man can miss God's timing, resulting in disaster.

Averting disaster requires understanding the vision and the time set for the purpose. Such avoidance brings about God's refuge and resourcefulness. God will always support his vision in you at the appointed time. So do not get ahead of God and yourself, wait on him!

Remember to utilize your time wisely:

'The opportunity of a lifetime must be seized within the lifetime of the opportunity.' - Leonard Ravenhill

ONE REFLECTION

What are the top three things you are planning to do soon (within the next year)? How much time do you think you will need for each one?

Chapter 5

IMPLEMENTING

"Knowledge is not power. Implementation of
knowledge is power."

- Larry Winget

The preceding chapters have sought to discuss our 'being'
before 'doing'. This following concept is advanced on the
premise of counting the cost before building on anything in
life. In this chapter the focus is on 'implementing' in life. This
occurs when we have a full understanding and sense of who
we are.

Implementing speaks of putting into practice what we
want to do through the knowledge we have acquired. It is

realising, employing and applying knowledge towards what we want to build, construct or establish. Implementing is when we put our plans for life into operation, service and action.

This is usually a process associated with stages in the management chain when administering a cause. When we implement a plan, we seek to manage that plan through people, information, and resources. Let us elaborate on the concept through a story from Nehemiah Chapter 4.

Nehemiah recognised that the cause of anything important must be attended to purposefully with urgency even if the conditions are imperfect. In his quest to rebuild Jerusalem, Nehemiah took responsibility for the task. He owned the project and drew on courage, vision and a strategy to make it happen. All this would amount to zero if he was unable to implement the plan with the knowledge he had. Nehemiah knew, leading his people in this endeavour, he was up against a renowned and formidable enemy, the Sanballat's threats of this world.

What he may have lacked in resources, equipment and tools, was made up in his resolve to rebuild, repair and reinvent God's mandate for Israel. In implementing such a plan, he encouraged men and women not to fear. He communicated unity of mind and purpose to build and to fight for their vision. Through division of labour, his forces were unified, disciplined and submitted in rank to the cause. Such was the great influence of a leader with a Godly cause. A vision is only as great as the sacrifice shown in its implementation of its plan. Even though the plan may not always be perfect, the cause is. In implementation of a plan, there is room for adjustments, improvements and changes.

As such Nehemiah was up to the task, with limited resources but with determined resolve. The restoration of Jerusalem was completed in 52 days, (no mean feat!), because they were united and had a mind to build. "Realize that a period of turmoil, while potentially a barrier to reform, may also present a unique opportunity." (Abraham Lincoln)

> But it so happened, when Sanballat heard that we were rebuilding the wall, that he was furious and very indignant, and mocked the Jews. And he spoke before his brethren and the army of Samaria, and said, "What are these feeble Jews doing? Will they fortify themselves? Will they offer sacrifices? Will they complete it in a day? Will they revive the stones from the heaps of rubbish—stones that are burned?"
> Now Tobiah the Ammonite was beside him, and he said, "Whatever they build, if even a fox goes up on it, he will break down their stone wall."
> Hear, O our God, for we are despised; turn their reproach on their own heads, and give them as plunder to a land of captivity! Do not cover their

iniquity, and do not let their sin be blotted out from before You; for they have provoked You to anger before the builders.

So we built the wall, and the entire wall was joined together up to half its height, for the people had a mind to work.

Now it happened, when Sanballat, Tobiah, the Arabs, the Ammonites, and the Ashdodites heard that the walls of Jerusalem were being restored and the [a]gaps were beginning to be closed, that they became very angry, and all of them conspired together to come and attack Jerusalem and create confusion. Nevertheless we made our prayer to our God, and because of them we set a watch against them day and night.

Then Judah said, "The strength of the laborers is failing, and there is so much rubbish that we are not able to build the wall."

And our adversaries said, "They will neither know nor see anything, till we come into their midst and kill them and cause the work to cease."

So it was, when the Jews who dwelt near them came, that they told us ten times, "From whatever place you turn, they will be upon us."

Therefore I positioned men behind the lower parts of the wall, at the openings; and I set the people according to their families, with their swords, their *spears, and their bows. And I looked, and arose and said to the nobles, to the leaders, and to the rest of the people, "Do not be afraid of them. Remember the Lord, great and awesome, and fight for your brethren, your sons, your daughters, your wives, and your houses."*

And it happened, when our enemies heard that it was known to us, and that God had brought their plot to nothing, that all of us returned to the wall, everyone to his work. So it was, from that time on, that half of my servants worked at construction, while the other half held the spears, the shields, the bows, and wore armor; and the leaders were behind all the house of Judah. Those who built on the wall, and those who carried burdens, loaded themselves so that with one hand they worked at construction, and with the other held a weapon. Every one of the builders had his sword girded at his side as he built. And the one who sounded the trumpet was beside me.

Then I said to the nobles, the rulers, and the rest of the people, "The work is great and extensive, and we are separated far from one another on the wall. Wherever you hear the sound of the trumpet, rally to us there. Our God will fight for us."

So we labored in the work, and half of [c]the men held the spears from daybreak until the stars appeared. At the same time I also said to the people, "Let each man and his servant stay at night in Jerusalem, that they may be our guard by night and a working party by day." So neither I, my brethren, my servants, nor the men of the guard who followed me took off our clothes, except that everyone took them off for washing. (Nehemiah 4)

OPPOSITION

Nehemiah had miraculous provision, divine commission to the task, and there was much prayer and fasting. However, all these things did not eliminate tough opposition. Tobiah and Sanballat were the archenemies of not only the project but the Jews as a people. They set themselves to mobilise opposition and used dirty tactics.

They ridiculed, distracted and spread malicious rumours. Nehemiah, however, was manifesting his 'being'! There is no way of stopping a vision whose time has come. The more trouble they sought to stir up, the more determined he became. The appropriate response was, as always, prayer.

LIMITED RESOURCES

When we tackle our mandate in its time, there will always be provision. God never assigns a vision without provision, but this process needs trust. As Reinhard Bonnke loved to say, 'Where God guides, He provides!'

We must walk by faith and know that he who has begun a good work in us will keep at it until its completion. There are times when we might feel discouraged and low, but God wants us in those times to look to him. He is the one who renews our strength as we wait on him.

TEAM DYNAMICS

When you are discharging your orders, God will give you people whose own mandate taps into yours. This makes you a leader not merely of a project, but of a team. A principal strength of any team is its dynamics. Some members are strong, others struggling. Some are mature while others are still growing but each one has a unique contribution to make.

Opposition is an attempt to break this team synergy. Sometimes team members feel they have nothing to contribute because they are not like the others. Nehemiah understood this and constantly evaluated the morale and motivation of his charges. Jesus had a team with good dynamics but constantly encouraged and defended them and affirmed them. When their time came to take over the mandate, they did not disappoint.

WHAT IS AT STAKE

Teams thrive on relationships. Nehemiah made it crystal clear that what was at stake was not the brick and mortar project they were embarking on but their people. He charged them to remember why they are doing it. It was a fight for their brethren, their sons and their daughters, their wives and their houses. People will do anything for their own. It is the leader's job to connect the dots.

DETERMINATION

Those who push against the opposition and succeed in manifesting what they have become, do so not in the absence of opposition and hardship, but in spite of it. Nehemiah's builders were also soldiers. They were not going to leave the work because of the enemy. Their determination meant hard work and long hours – but that is what progress is made of!

STRATEGY

Nehemiah was not a random builder. He was not just a gritty guy slogging away for long hours! He had a strategy, a clear long-term plan that allowed him to make the decisions about the opposition, the internal issues and how the whole community had to relate to God. We see this in Jesus. He also had a clear goal in mind and he organised his life around that. He was absolutely clear about the choices of people, places and actions that furthered his goals.

A critical factor to strategy is time. Successful people know they do not have forever to do their work. They are conscious of the limited time.

Nehemiah was key to God's plan and he knew he was called for such a time. The story is about the struggles Israel (God's people) faced when trying to rebuild the wall around Jerusalem. Nehemiah had a career as a politician. He was a governor. His leadership was characterised by the way he ruled with justice and righteousness. He was viewed as a man of integrity.

Nehemiah discovered the ruined state of Jerusalem from fellow Jews who had come from the city. He also recognised that Jerusalem was God's chosen city to propagate God's divine purpose. The call to action required Nehemiah to ask time off from his profession in the King's court to pursue God's vision.

Nehemiah recognised that the rebuilding of God's vision of Jerusalem was needed. He sought God's plan through prayer, counsel and wisdom before he went about its implementation. Nehemiah had within him the capacity to do this because through his vocation he had matured in leadership, vision, character and integrity.

Once he was up-to-date on the extent of the destruction of Jerusalem, he formulated a plan for restoration and presented it to the King in Susa. The King granted Nehemiah a concession to return to Jerusalem, with the mandate to rebuild the city's perimeter wall. However, Jerusalem not only needed physical rebuilding. Her people were also backslidden in their evil ways.

Jerusalem at the time needed restoration through a God-breathed plan. This is a characteristic of God – he reveals his will through the types and shadows of the past. This amazing story is a type or shadow of Jesus returning to a restored and spotless bride, the Church.

Nehemiah discovered that non-Jews were permitted to conduct business inside Jerusalem on the Sabbath and to keep rooms in the Temple. This was a transgression that was a shame to Jerusalem.

This incensed Nehemiah, who purified the Temple and the Levitical Priests. He went on further to enforce and restore the observance of the Mosaic Laws.

Nehemiah fought for what he believed God had given him and the people of Jerusalem. He did not renege on the task of fighting for what he was not willing to lose.

The implementation of this plan to restore Jerusalem to its fear of God required commitment and dedication. It required not only Nehemiah but also the Jewish nation to accomplish this feat.

Leading Israel's forces, Nehemiah sought to rebuild the walls of Jerusalem. Together as a nation they encountered challenges and difficulties at various stages. They were discouraged, threatened and criticized by their opponents, namely Sanballat and Tobiah.

Nevertheless, they constantly withstood the torment of their adversaries. United in purpose, with a vision that was in line with God's Word, they overcame their enemies. It is interesting that the initial battle was the enemy within themselves but having repented, they were able to withstand their adversaries.

This plan of action could only be implemented by a group of people who understood who they were in God, a people who carried the character of God. Furthermore, they were a people who had the ability and will to do what God required.

I believe Nehemiah understood the times and the Lord's visitation on Israel. He was equipped with God's skill set to carry out the God-designed plan. It took Nehemiah having a relationship bathed in prayer before he could implement God's vision. God seeks men and women who make themselves available.

The fulfilment of God's plan brought about the restoration of Jerusalem. Jerusalem has always been central to God's vision for what happens globally, hence, the importance of keeping Jerusalem intact.

What can we learn from the implementation of Nehemiah's plan in restoring God's vision? I believe vision is from God. It is made up of leadership through influence gained in what we do daily in our vocation; it has the character of God because we choose his ways not our own; it walks in integrity by standing for the truth in the Word.

LIFE'S LESSONS

My personal encounter with implementing God's plan is being absorbed into every facet of my life. Of course, all aspects are important but one area seems to stand out for me – the issue of integrity. This facet consumes me and constantly challenges my very being.

In this respect, I have come to realise that integrity is not necessarily being right. I believe integrity is being transparently truthful, the measure being God's Word. In the wake of error, it is the ability to put your hand up and assume responsibility. This is irrespective of the consequences of the error.

The Word gives us the wisdom, instruction and understanding for godly living. Implementation of this God-honouring living requires that we execute and discharge God's principles no matter what the cost.

Buy the truth, and sell it not; also wisdom, and instruction, and understanding. (Proverbs 23:23)

My fascination with the above scripture, speaks daily to our lives. We are admonished to purchase things that seem intangible in order to demonstrate tangibility in our daily lives. Scripture at times can seem so far removed from the context of our lives that it appears irrelevant. Yet scripture not only is relevant but fundamental and profound.

I live in a country and continent where bribery threatens the moral fibre of my people. We complain about the rampant increase of crime and immorality, yet collectively we sponsor and fuel this pain in our respective societies.

Once, while driving to repair my vehicle, a friend called on my mobile phone. I took the call with the knowledge that having a handset glued to one's ear while driving is prohibited. I proceeded to talk until a traffic policeman saw me and flagged me down.

This encounter was embarrassing for me as I consider myself an advocate for integrity. The policeman seemed excited at having caught me. I profusely apologised for my transgression. Here is the real deal – was I really sorry for what I did, or was I sorry for being caught?

Prior to being caught by the policeman, I must confess that I had been doing this for some time. I had heard the jingle of the numerous advertisements over radio and television regarding the dangers of speaking on the cellphone whilst driving. The result of such a transgression is a fine.

The policeman was quick to summon me to his car, where he asked me to 'talk to him'. You must understand this term 'talk to him' meant that if you do not want to receive a written traffic offense ticket it would be in your best interest to pay a bribe.

My mind raced between God's way of living and copping out the worldly, easy way. Sanity prevailed with my insistence for the officer to write out the ticket. Looking at him, I saw the expression of disappointment clearly etched on his face. Yes, I know the punishable offense is far more than the bribe, but I also know I am answerable to a state God approves of.

Because of who I am in Christ I have also learnt what to do. I dared not become a statistic of corruption of self, God and the state. I denied the devil and his cohorts the pleasure of further sponsoring the corruption of God's property, Man.

When we corrupt or are corrupted a little, we then carry the potential to become corrupt or corrupted a great deal. What then? We are called to be implementers of God's designed way of living, and that simply is the truth. No excuses, no ducking or diving, the buck must stop with you.

Why is this matter such a pre-occupation with me? Just like Nehemiah, God may use me as an instrument to reach out and restore His people. Just think, what would happen if God were to send the very same traffic policeman to a meeting where I am called to minister the Word of God?

The traffic officer may be coming to receive his day of salvation from the Lord. My lack of integrity may hinder him from receiving from God. May grace abound as we seek to implement God's way of living here on earth.

My point is that we cannot implement God's vision without embracing His character in our lives. We must become like Christ and also do like Christ. Today, church, society and communities carry the challenge of being like Christ.

I have not always got it right. On my recent trip to renew our passports, I encountered a similar incident of bribery. My friends wanted to help by having an internal officer at the passport office expedite this transaction.

Although I was unaware of the goings on, I must say I was not entirely naïve of the possibility of clandestine activity. I played along with the plan as I had limited time before going back to work. Submission of the application forms were made at the official rate as advertised by the passport office.

However, I then learnt an additional amount of USD100 was added for services rendered. I knew immediately that this was bribe money for the passports to be expedited. As the applications were already in the system, I endured a sleepless night. I tossed and turned wondering how I could have become entangled in this mess.

First and foremost, I spoke to God and I repented of my transgression. I decided to take responsibility. I had placed my interest ahead of that of the passport officer. How? I decided to place value on my needs at the expense of exploiting another human being.

I became an accomplice who sponsored an illegal act, a bribe. The officer had a different point of view, as I will explain. The following morning, I sought the audience of the passport officer via friends who had initiated the transaction.

My meeting with the officer made my friends nervous. Nevertheless, they facilitated the meeting and I proceeded to apologise to the officer for having placed a higher premium on my need at the expense of his life.

I also realised that the officer was a professing Christian. I was alarmed by his response. It typified the culture of doing business in a manner contrary to principles, ethics and ethos.

The officer did not quite understand why I was harping on about this issue; rather, he pointed out that what was happening was a daily occurrence. He felt this was a viable means of making money, boastfully mentioning that a tithe would be raised for the church for such 'work'.

My deliberation with the officer focused on my being principled. In short, after my long-winded apology, I said that since the clandestine payment may have been consumed that I would 'technically' retain it and offer it back to the officer as a seed.

This surprised the officer. I advised him that prospering in the Lord requires *HIS* way of doing things. My encouragement was that the 'seed' be a tangible point. Thereafter the officer would no longer do business in this manner. The thinking was it would afford us the opportunity to believe God to prosper the officer in a credible manner.

The officer seemed to only vaguely understand this form of repentance. Rather, he was more concerned with the possibility of my 'spilling the beans' to his superiors. I assured him that this would not be the case but I took time to encourage him to stop the clandestine way of soliciting money and instead look to God to provide.

Thereafter, we amicably parted ways having repented with the hope that in future such a matter would be avoided. All this happened in the presence of friends who were privy to the whole matter. Had I been wrong? Oh, yes, I also chose to take responsibility through repentance and bring forth the truth of God' Word.

Even when we miss it, there is always God's plan for implementing His truth. This will always create a righteous way forward that separates one from condemnation and sin.

Again, just like the previous example of the traffic policeman, there may just be an opportunity to minister to the passport officer in the future. I believe this sets us up to becoming honourable vessels to minister effectively in the future.

ONE REFLECTION

Draw up a simple plan of action to achieve a personal goal in your life in the next year. This should include resources, relationships, activities and places, all centered around the goal.

Chapter 6

FRUITION

"The pain of discipline is short, but the glory of
fruition is eternal."

- Harriet Beecher Stowe

An instruction is the solution to obedience. Obedience or the
lack thereof will always bear fruit. Fruition is the completion
or fulfilment of the seeds we sow in life. Fruition is an
achievement of a defined life cycle of obedience to a specific
instruction.

Fruition will always require compliance, conformity and
agreement to a set order or process. It is never achieved at
random nor without due process. Yet it is potentially in every

seed. God operates by processes and instructions, expecting obedience to generate fruition.

Fruition comes as a result of the ideal tuition of processed knowledge. Knowledge is the information, facts and data required enroute to a desired and purposed outcome. Simply put, sowing a mango seed should result in a mango tree. The tree should produce mangoes not apples.

What is sown is what is reaped. Everything that is sown originates from a seed. A seed will carry the DNA or characteristics potentially directed towards 'fruition'. Seed is always the starting point of the possibility of a harvest, yield, and produce, or in business terms, a return on investment.

The above is my attempt to explain fruition in light of 'being' and or 'becoming' in order to 'do' effectively. It is therefore imperative to realise the importance of being a seed in life. Biologically we start off as a sperm that interacts with an ovum in conception. We are incubated before birth. At birth we carry the potential anatomical attributes of a fully developed person.

The gap from birth to maturity of man's anatomy follows a developmental path. That path demands elements required toward maturity. For example, the diet will change periodically depending on the requirements for development. Notably, a baby will not consume solid food until it is ready to take on solids. Vitamins and value-added food are different in form at each stage of development.

The standard formula for sowing and reaping fruit is as follows:

You reap *what* you sow.

You reap *later* than you sow.

You reap *more* than you sow.

This pattern stresses the relationship between the seed and the fruit. You cannot do what you are not! If you do, then you are only a hollow approximation of what you really can be. The second element speaks to the process that it takes to move from the seed, to the fruit. Nothing happens overnight in the Kingdom.

Even when something looks instant, it has been in the process for a long time, waiting to manifest itself in its time. The last element speaks to the abundance of the potential. Jesus always used tiny symbols to illustrate the potency of the Kingdom of God. He said it was like the mustard seed, like the yeast in a batch of dough or a lamp on a stand.

Just as each developmental point carries 'seed' towards fruition, spiritually the principle is the same. Christian spirituality requires the Word of God as nourishment for development. This perpetuates the expectation of growth and maturity. As a Christian develops in his or her path, other dimensions are introduced for effectiveness, such as prayer, character and purpose among other things.

Going back to the concept of 'becoming' before 'doing', there is a realisation of a developmental path for effective living. The starting point is always an initiator for growth. The path of development requires adequate nourishment for optimum growth. This growth is geared toward a desired fruition for purposeful living.

The fruit emerges out of the seed and if nourished and tended well, all the potential of being is manifest in the doing!

Sometimes one is unable to reach optimum levels in effective living because of a lack of adequate nourishment, not only physically but in every area of life. Fruition demands that adequate resources be utilized in the developmental path.

Even the life span of a business will require adequate management of people, information and resources for sustainability. What is noteworthy is the emphasis placed on years in school before one can embark on a life's vocation purposefully. Shouldn't the same emphasis be placed on our spiritual growth?

Amazingly, we do not look for fruit from an immature tree. Yet, sometimes we are out of our depth as immature individuals, trying to do stuff that requires maturity beyond the return of investment. Basically, what we put in is what we get out; anything beyond this is likely to be a lottery.

I believe it is time to recognise the pattern Jesus embarked on. A thirty-year investment in preparation followed by a three and a half year executed ministry that revolutionized the world. This is the fruition that we as individuals should aspire to – Jesus, our wonderful example!

Even so, every good tree bears good fruit, but a bad tree bears bad fruit. A good tree cannot bear bad fruit, nor can a bad tree bear good fruit. Every tree that does not bear good fruit is cut down and thrown into the fire. Therefore by their fruits you will know them. Not everyone who says to Me, 'Lord, Lord,' shall enter the kingdom of heaven, but he who does the will of My Father in heaven. (Matthew 7:17-21)

In the context of the Word of God, the Father seeks to perpetuate fruitfulness through his kingdom. The Apostle Matthew speaks about a tree not only bearing fruit, but qualifies the quality or lack thereof. While he does not mention the quality of the seed, he is at pains to describe the quality of the tree – a good tree or a bad one.

Then God said, "Let the earth bring forth grass, the herb that yields   seed, and the fruit   tree that yields fruit according to its kind, whose seed is in itself, on the earth"; and it was so. And the earth brought forth grass, the herb that yields seed according to its kind, and the tree that yields fruit, whose seed is in itself according to its kind. And God saw that it was good. (Genesis 1:11-12)

God initiated the principle of trees yielding fruit after its kind. This means that a seed was designed to qualify the quality of its potential yield. Going back to our initial example of a mango tree bearing mangoes, we can substantiate that seed gives produce after its kind.

Following the seed-harvest principle, the seed determines what the outcome is for the produce. Generally, a bad seed produces a bad harvest. Or at times a potentially good seed can be negatively influenced by the bad nourishment it receives.

In other words, a mango seed if not nourished by the right ingredients, can fail to yield good fruit. Maybe the seed did not receive adequate water, nutrition and vital components necessary for growth, so having an impact on its ability to yield fruit.

When a seed matures into a tree, it ought to have a reputation of bearing quality fruit. Fruition in life is not limited to multiplicity, but can be fruitfulness, meaning the ability to replenish, subdue and dominate. Fruition of purpose in humans speaks of status, reputation and character in life.

God spoke to Man at the beginning and commanded the quality of fruit from Man which he was looking for as noted in the text below:

> Then God said, "Let Us make man in Our image, according to Our likeness; let them have dominion over the fish of the sea, over the birds of the air, and over the cattle, over [a]all the earth and over every creeping thing that creeps on the earth." So God created man in His own image; in the image of God He created him; male and female He created them. Then God blessed them, and God said to them, "Be fruitful and multiply; fill the earth and subdue it; have dominion over the fish of the sea, over the birds of the air, and over every living thing that [b]moves on the earth." (Genesis 1:26-28)

Man is God's seed with God's expression regarding the quality of that seed. Sowed in an environment conducive to growth, that seed will produce after its kind. Thus, the Kingdom of God was crafted and designed to perpetuate and propagate in the same way.

In another passage of scripture, the Apostle John speaks of fruition in a collective manner. He uses the analogy of

Christ being the tree and the branches being effective disciples called to produce fruit. The inability of ineffective branches to effectively produce fruit results in the pruning of such branches.

> *Every branch in Me that does not bear fruit He takes away; and every branch that bears fruit He prunes, that it may bear more fruit. You are already clean because of the word which I have spoken to you. Abide in Me, and I in you. As the branch cannot bear fruit of itself, unless it abides in the vine, neither can you, unless you abide in Me. I am the vine, you are the branches. He who abides in Me, and I in him, bears much fruit; for without Me you can do nothing. If anyone does not abide in Me, he is cast out as a branch and is withered; and they gather them and throw them into the fire, and they are burned. If you abide in Me, and My words abide in you, you will ask what you desire, and it shall be done for you. (John 15:2-7)*

God is clear about his expectation of fruition in respect of his seed. He has provided every possible means of making sure this is possible. This is done via his incorruptible precious Word. The necessary nourishment required is made available in the Word.

LIFE'S LESSONS

I have experienced the pleasure of an opportunity of being a pioneer of an exceptional work. What I noticed in the growth of this work is clarity of principled applications tested from time immemorial. I can attest to the fact that the work showed remarkable results after a protracted period.

The initial growth was not visible. Neither was it always tangible to start off with. However, the consistent and constant application of the principle of seed-harvest eventually bore the desired fruit.

I have been part of a church ministry for almost 20 years. Its history from inception now spans over three decades. The initial seed was only a handful of people. From humble beginnings, God has multiplied this to over thousands of people on numerous global locations. The impact has been a God-vision internationally.

As a young sportsman, I carried the dream of representing my country internationally in the sports arena. This state of bearing such fruit required sowing the seed that would produce this desired outcome. Disciplined training and a conducive environment helped achieve my goal.

The price of such representation demanded dedicated time and effort from the coaches and me. There were days I was flying like an eagle but there was also plenty opportunity to throw in the towel. It helped me understand the distinction between being trained and being taught the skills.

Anyone can be taught the skills; few have the substance to master the discipline of those taught skills. Training is preparation of the required skills daily until the skills become second nature to you.

Many are cautious when watching professionals perform, bemused by the exhilarating level of proficiency. I always appreciate the time it takes to perfect such skill sets. Special talent will always require a protracted period of training to be a winner.

The adage says, 'Practice makes perfect', I also like the saying, 'Practice makes permanent'. So, guided by the incomparable Book of Life, the Bible, the more we are trained regarding Christian life principles, potentially, the greater the outcome of having the Christ-like life.

The return on investment regarding successful Christian living calls for first 'becoming in Christ' and then 'doing in Christ'. It will always require paying a price. At times it will not only demand inspiration but also perspiration! Life requires effort and commitment – no matter the cost.

There is no easy formula; no 'easy come, easy go'. To get on top of your game it will require 'hard graft'. The Apostle Paul understood that in his calling he would endure blood, sweat and tears. I am sure anything worth pursuing carries a massive price tag. Are you willing to pay the price?

I believe my earlier days in sport helped create a foundation that has provided me with certain privileges in life. It held me in good stead when I was given the opportunity to run a national sporting academy for my country. It afforded me the privilege of coaching future talents in various sporting disciplines.

Through my acquired sporting prowess, I also had the privilege of travelling well over three quarters of the world as a sportsman, sports administrator and coach. Recently, this earlier impact has resulted in my involvement in a business environment. This space works with consultants, integral coaches and business developers in the world of business.

Since I learnt to be trained, I am now in a situation where I train others in life. I had an opportunity to be pastored before I was ordained a pastor, with one of my life's vocations being Itinerary Teaching Ministry. I shared my personal experiences with you so you would firstly appreciate the giftings God has made available to me. Secondly, I shared this to demonstrate what is possible through sheer determination, commitment and dedication–. Thirdly, it gives you an idea of where this 'fella' is coming from.

ONE REFLECTION

In this chapter there is a standard formula for sowing and reaping. Describe how you are sowing or have sown and your expectation for a harvest?

Chapter 7

REWARD

"Faith is to believe what you do not see; the reward of this
faith is to see what you believe."

- Saint Augustine

In psychology, reward is a process that reinforces behaviour.
Hold that thought for a while. Reward can also be viewed as
an offered incentive. Reward can range from remuneration,
compensation and bonus just to name a few examples. The
antonym of reward is penalty, punishment and fine.

Going back to reward being a process; this stems from
the view of reward being a conditional transaction, the
notion being if one fulfils a desired request, reward is duly

expected. Simply put, we receive to the measure of what we put in. Our efforts for the work we do are duly rewarded.

Since we are rewarded for the problems we solve in life, the complexity of the problem attracts a higher reward. Reward is a godly principle. It is the satisfaction of a fulfillment of God's purpose that manifests reward. In other words, reward can be a by-product of obedience to God's purpose.

> *And, behold, I come quickly; and my reward is with me, to give every man according as his work shall be. (Revelation 22:12)*

Reward is the outcome of fulfilling a purposeful request. I also believe it is a manifestation of a desirable fulfillment or solution to a request or problem. Reward is unique in that it is only administered when a solution has been provided that has an impact on a desired outcome.

Jesus spoke at length about reward. He mentioned the Father openly rewarding his faithful children for Godly deeds done privately. He also spoke of how hypocrites that seek to be rewarded would lose their reward. It seems that the aftermath of obedience is reward. And, reward is not only reserved for heaven but also here on earth. Jesus spoke clearly in this regard.

Rejoice and be exceedingly glad, for great is your reward in heaven, for so they persecuted the prophets who were before you. (Matthew 5:12)

Rejoice in that day and leap for joy! For indeed your reward is great in heaven, For in like manner their fathers did to the prophets. (Luke 6:23)

But you, when you pray, go into your room, and when you have shut your door, pray to your Father who is in the secret place; and your Father who sees in secret will reward you [a]openly. (Matthew 6:6)

For the Scripture says, "You shall not muzzle an ox while it treads out the grain," and, "The laborer is worthy of his wages." (1 Timothy 5:18)

These few scriptures teach us that whether here on earth or heaven, we will be rewarded for obedience to God's purpose. Our response to God's requests through his Word will determine how we are rewarded. A negative response will attract negativity regarding reward. There seems to be an exception when it comes to the following:

Behold, children are a heritage from the LORD,
The fruit of the womb is a reward. (Psalm 127:3)

God is Sovereign, who gracefully provides a fruitful womb as a reward. This reward is not conditional but via grace. Just like salvation is made available to humanity, not because of our works but by grace through faith.

> So the men of Israel said, "Have you seen this man who has come up? Surely he has come up to defy Israel; and it shall be that the man who kills him the king will enrich with great riches, will give him his daughter, and give his father's house exemption from taxes in Israel."
> Then David spoke to the men who stood by him, saying, "What shall be done for the man who kills this Philistine and takes away the reproach from Israel? For who is this uncircumcised Philistine, that he should defy the armies of the living God?"
> And the people answered him in this manner, saying, "So shall it be done for the man who kills him."
> Now Eliab his oldest brother heard when he spoke to the men; and Eliab's anger was aroused against David, and he said, "Why did you come down here? And with whom have you left those few sheep in the wilderness? I know your pride and the insolence of your heart, for you have come down to see the battle."
> And David said, "What have I done now? Is[a] there not a cause?" Then he turned from him toward another and said the same thing; and these people answered him as the first ones did. Now when the words which David spoke were heard, they

reported them to Saul; and he sent for him. (1 Samuel 17:25-31)

In the salvation of Israel during the crisis of Goliath and the Philistines, David sought a personal reward. I think that for every corporate challenge, solving such challenges will always bring about a personal reward. David was personally rewarded; however, the main purpose was God used David to liberate a nation from its adversary.

What David clearly understood about reward was that it must be born out of purpose. His preparation in fighting and overcoming a bear and a lion stood him in good stead in the conquest of his giant, Goliath. When his preparation for the fight encountered the opportunity, he was up to the task.

As I draw on David's story, I cannot help but return to the theme, 'being' before 'doing'. David became a winning warrior before the day of reckoning. He built up resolve within himself that exhibited courage, tenacity and a 'no retreat no surrender' quality.

David became a winning warrior internally before he took on the giant. He was a personal success as a warrior without the audience of Israel. He merely expressed that 'x-factor' of conquest through the skill he had mastered privately by bringing it into the public domain against Goliath of Gath.

Personally, I have found that reward is first gained in the privacy of our daily lives and then made manifest publicly for God's glory. Therefore, the success of our daily private life will invariably influence and impact how we are rewarded publicly.

> *"Take heed that you do not do your charitable deeds before men, to be seen by them. Otherwise you have no reward from your Father in heaven.*
>
> *Therefore, when you do a charitable deed, do not sound a trumpet before you as the hypocrites do in the synagogues and in the streets, that they may have glory from men. Assuredly, I say to you, they have their reward. But when you do a charitable deed, do not let your left hand know what your right hand is doing, that your charitable deed may be in secret; and your Father who sees in secret will Himself reward you [a]openly.*
>
> *"And when you pray, you shall not be like the hypocrites. For they love to pray standing in the synagogues and on the corners of the streets, that they may be seen by men. Assuredly, I say to you, they have their reward. But you, when you pray, go into your room, and when you have shut your door, pray to your Father who is in the secret place; and your Father who sees in secret will reward you [c]openly. And when you pray, do not use vain*

repetitions as the heathen do. For they think that they
will be heard for their many words." (Matthew 6:1-7)

God's investment in Man is designed to bear a harvest based on the fruitful Word of God. Obedience to his Word is Man's reward. Emphatically, the Word is Our Saviour Jesus Christ, who is our reward of salvation for eternity. Therefore, life in Christ is our daily reward. In him we attain a promised reward daily.

LIFE'S LESSONS

I was accustomed to thinking that being rewarded was always conditional on me doing something. This was until I realised Christ gifted and rewarded me unconditionally with eternal life. The onus is on me to accept this exceptional gift and reward.

His unconditional love is my reward in life and it is not dependent on what I can do. I have been gifted with a redeemed life through Christ. This relationship with Christ is mutual. This reciprocal relationship is a bond for eternity. God is also not confined to a box of rules regarding rewarding people.

...with goodwill doing service, as to the Lord, and not
to men, knowing that whatever good anyone does, he

will receive the same from the Lord, whether he is a slave or free. (Ephesians 6:7-8)

God will reward everyone for the things that they do.

After these things the word of the LORD came to Abram in a vision, saying, "Do not be afraid, Abram. I am your shield, your exceedingly great reward." (Genesis 15:1)

If God could be Abram's reward, how much more can He be mine! He is my exceeding great reward – in actual fact, heaven is not my reward, God is. It just happens that God resides in heaven. Therefore, I am destined to appear before him at his residence, so that I can continue enjoying him as my reward, eternally.

In my life, God is an Infinite Reward. This means he is boundless, unlimited and endless. As my reward, I received him not by merit. Limited as I was, how did I receive an Unlimited God? This can only be via an Unlimited Mediator, Jesus Christ.

I find it amazing that as a previously limited being I have received an Unlimited God. Just imagine an imperfect being with a Perfect God. Infinite God living in finite Kudzai, how awesome is this? Only his divine mercy and grace affords me the merit of him as my reward.

The LORD is my shepherd; I shall not want. He makes me to lie down in green pastures; He leads me beside the still waters. He restores my soul; He leads me in the paths of righteousness for His name's sake. Yea, though I walk through the valley of the shadow of death, I will fear no evil; For You are with me; Your rod and Your staff, they comfort me. You prepare a table before me in the presence of my enemies; You anoint my head with oil; My cup runs over.
Surely goodness and mercy shall follow me all the days of my life; And I will dwell in the house of the LORD Forever. (Psalm 23:1-6)

David, a man after God's heart, wrote Psalm 23. He beautifully describes his relationship with Father God. God is the source of David's reward. God is all sufficient in every situation in his life. What did David do to deserve God as his reward?

As I look at the relationships between God and the men and women of God in the Bible, I see clearly how they have a need for God. This must be the ultimate reward Man can receive here on earth for eternity. My desire is to live fully aware of the spiritual reality of God being my daily reward. What more do I want? Knowing that an 'Infinite Reward' lives in my innermost being is an awesome privilege, not only in this life but for eternity.

ONE REFLECTION

How does understanding that God is both your reward and rewarder spur you on in your quest to live a life of purpose?

CONCLUSION

In the heart of every human being, yourself included, is a desire to connect with meaning and purpose. We desire to express something that is beyond the biological. We crave for meaning beyond our education, jobs and possessions that we acquire. We know that there is more to life than philosophy, politics and religion.

Often however, many of us find that 'thing' elusive and hard to obtain. It is true that you cannot find it here or there, because that 'thing' is the Kingdom of God. Jesus said the Kingdom of God does not come in visible form, but that it is within us. This is the state where God rules our hearts and manifests the substance that He put in us from the inside going outward!

In closing, I need to repeat that this can only be a reality through a relationship with God. He has made this possible by reaching out to us first, through Jesus Christ.

For God so loved the world that he gave his one and only Son, that whoever believes in him shall not perish but have eternal life. For God did not send his Son into the world to condemn the world, but to save the world through him. Whoever believes in him is not condemned, but whoever does not believe stands condemned already because he has not believed in the name of God's one and only Son. (John 3: 16-18, NIV)

If we are to have any hope of leaving an indelible mark here, we must put our trust in him and respond to his gracious love towards us, by faith and with deep gratitude. Then only can we effectively 'do' God's Kingdom bidding.

It is futile for man to 'do' much on earth without becoming a 'being' in God. 'Doing' life without 'being' in God is an inappropriate way of living. Why?

Jesus said to him, "I am the way, the truth, and the life. No one comes to the Father except through Me." (John 14:6)

If I try to live by any other way, truth or life than the Lord Jesus Christ, I will be left grasping at a disastrous eternal life separated from the Father. My desire is that my encouragement, conviction and persuasion will provoke you to becoming God's 'being' as you pursue 'doing' kingdom bidding.

I can do all things through Christ who strengthens me. (Philippians 4:13)

Let the words of Apostle Paul propel you to the transformation from independence, leaning on self, to dependence on Christ in everything you do.

PRAYER OF SALVATION

I invite you to pray this prayer for salvation. As you read this prayer, make it your personal prayer as you speak these words from the very depths of your heart. On completion of this prayer, you will be born again into the family of Almighty God:

> *Heavenly Father, in the Name of Jesus, I come to you. I thank you that you said that if I come to you, you will not cast me out, and that you said "Everyone who calls upon the name of the Lord shall be saved" (Romans 10:13). I call upon you to save me Lord Jesus.*
>
> *According to Romans 10:9-10, I confess with my mouth that you are Lord and believe in my heart that you were raised from the dead. Forgive me of all my sin, cleanse me and make me whole; come into my heart and be Lord over my life. I believe right now that I am saved and I say: 'I am born again and I am a child of Almighty God, in the name of Jesus.' Amen*

THE BAPTISM OF THE HOLY SPIRIT

Now, thank God for making you his child and ask him to baptise you with the Holy Spirit.

Pray this prayer:
Heavenly Father, I am a believer. I am Your child and You are my Father. Jesus is my Lord. I believe with all my heart that Your Word is true. You said that if I ask, I will receive the Holy Spirit.
So, in the Name of Jesus Christ, my Lord, please fill me to overflowing with Your precious Holy Spirit. Father baptize me in the Holy Spirit. Because of Your Word, I believe that I now receive. Thank You! I believe the Holy Spirit is within me and, by faith, I accept it.
Now, Holy Spirit, rise up within me as I praise God. I fully expect to speak with other tongues, as You give me the utterance.

Now begin giving sound to the expressions in your heart. Speak and hear the Holy Spirit speaking through you.

Rejoice! You have just been baptized in the Holy Spirit! You have been filled with power—Hallelujah!

Important Scripture References:
Luke 11:10 -13, Acts 2:4, Jude 20,1 Corinthians 14:4

ACKNOWLEDGEMENTS

I would like to thank my family, friends and business partners for encouraging me to pursue my dreams. What a blessing to be around people who challenge and inspire me to be tenacious! This book is not only a realisation of my vision but also a reflection of the great support I received during this writing process.

After my debut book, *Faith*, it is my honour and pleasure to put this book into your hands. An assignment of this magnitude would not be possible without God's guidance which has been wonderfully complemented by the unconditional support of my wife and children.

I have also benefitted immensely from the generosity of others in accomplishing this feat. Ministers of the Gospel who relentlessly study God's Word have helped shape and fashion my thinking.

The unfolding of the precious lives of my extended family, friends and acquaintances, continue to teach me. I truly appreciate the lessons gleaned from watching your precious lives unfold.

My gratitude and thanks go to everyone who has laboured in assisting me with editorial work and the 'slog' behind the scenes. Special mention must be made to my Executive

Editor, Pastor Evangeline van den Berg for her tireless effort and professional input. To the publishing consultant, Pastor Niq Sibanda together with James Nondo, special thanks!

And to those who choose to read this book – please ccelebrate with me! I trust 'Being before Doing' will be a blessing and encouragement to you.

Warmest regards and blessings,

Kudzai

Thank you all!